Advance Praise for *Victim No More!*

Who would have thought that karate and Christianity had anything in common?! Shauna has found the similarities of empowerment, discipline and spiritual centering. Frank lessons are followed by challenging journal questions. A unique resource.

Bettijane Burger, workshop participant and retired teacher.

By page 4 I knew I wanted this book in the hands of my daughters. By the end of the first lesson I had mentally made my Christmas List and plan to order by the case. Then halfway through something strange happened. I began to think that this book might just help me too! I truly learned from reading Shauna's book.

I think this book can be helpful to all walks. I so enjoyed her comparison to Karate, it kept it not only interesting but very practical. At the end of each chapter you have picture words to remind you of the lessons. I do not know all that the author has been through but I do know that the passion with which she writes comes from true pain and agony.

Deb Copeland, Author of *Attitude Therapy*, motivational speaker, www.debcopeland.com

I recommend *Victim No More* to all readers. Many persons, men, women and children have been neglected and abused by life experiences. Shauna Hyde, an effective and gifted pastor, has provided a useful resource to all who have been wounded by life to enable them to move on to a full and happy life.

Bishop William Boyd Grove
United Methodist Church, Retired

I commend this book to God's pilgrim disciples who earnestly desire to lead a new life immersed in the imperatives of Jesus' teachings. One's attention and interest are arrested immediately because the text unites the discipline of karate with the rigors of practicing one's spiritual disciplines. The reader is joyfully drawn into a fresh understanding of "what God does for us" while being motivated to become an inspired participant in God's activity in one's life. We see how victims of life's painful circumstances can be transformed into victorious living in Jesus Christ.

Bishop Ernest S. Lyght,
The West Virginia Area,
The United Methodist Church

I have known Shauna for quite a few years and her devotion to God and the martial arts and to helping others are her life. I can see she wrote from her heart and her love of God. She was able to bring both together in a very special and spiritual way.

Don Madden, Soke of Kosetumi Seiei Kahn,
former US Olympic Karate Coach

Despair is a dark and lonely prison cell, sealed by a door with hinges that rust shut almost as soon as the reverberations of its closing die away. In *Victim No More*, Shauna offers insights through her own journey that offer help and hope for those who also know the darkness as well as those who need tips for spiritual and emotional wholeness. "Learn to see past the problem," is her advice to consider right before advocating a karate kick to that rusted door. The book's format makes it a great tool for individuals or study groups. Thanks Shauna!

Rev. Dr. Gary E. Nelson
United Methodist pastor
Fellow in the American Association of Pastoral Counselors
Author of
A Relentless Hope: Surviving the Storm of Teen Depression

This is the most extraordinary book I have ever read. It is very rare to find a woman martial-arts master and more rare to meet a woman martial-arts master and pastor! Such a person is Rev. Hyde who beautifully juxtaposes and contrasts Christian discipleship and Karate martial arts to bring out values and beauties in them. Transformed from being a victim of domestic violence to a UMC pastor and inductee of the International Black Belt Hall of Fame, she is a truly inspirational and authentic human being in the making. Full of spiritual instructions and practical wisdom, this book will make a person spiritually and physically fit and ready for life challenges. It is a trailblazing book. Highly recommended!

Andrew S. Park
Professor of Theology and Ethics
United Theological Seminary, Dayton, OH

This book offers a wholly original, body-mind-spirit approach to the damage of domestic violence. Shauna Hyde has, in fact, crafted a doable, Wesleyan, spiritual regimen for Christians recovering from any form of overwhelming despair. Even when I had questions about the metaphor of fighting, the sense of hope Hyde conveys is irresistable.

Traci C. West, Professor of Ethics and African American Studies, Drew University

Victim No More!

Shauna Hyde

Energion Publications
www.energionpubs.com

2011

Author photo courtesy of Steven Holsclaw.

ISBN10: 1-893729-96-6
ISBN13: 978-1-893729-96-4
Library of Congress Control Number: 2011934186

Energion Publications
P.O. Box 841
Gonzalez, FL 32560

(850) 525-3916
energionpubs.com

Acknowledgments

I have been blessed in life to be able to say that there are many people along the way who have believed in me. To my family, I say thank you. My parents, siblings, in-laws, nieces, nephews, etc. have comprised a wonderful family who have always done their best to do what is right and have always loved each other no matter what.

My husband, Wayne Hollandsworth, has the ability to be married to me and that says something!

The list of specific names is difficult to do because there are always so many people in life who are a positive influence. Due to the nature of this book I have narrowed it down to the United Methodist Church and Ko Sutemi Seiei Kahn Karate and the folks in those organizations for whom I am deeply grateful.

UNITED METHODIST CHURCH:

Bishop Lyght – gave me a chance

Bishop Grove - encourages me

Dr Andrew Sung Park – exemplifies grace

Rev. Marilyn Schroeder – got me started!

KARATE:

Soke Don Madden – believes in me

Master Brent Bias – is patient with me

Sensei Lynn Lovell – encourages me

Sensei Denny and Angie Britton – got me started!

Gail and Carol Hopkins – push me to be more and believe in my ability to do it

My mentors and my instructors in seminary who encouraged me to write down what I was thinking and then seek publication.

Joel Watts who was the key that unlocked the door!

Energion Publications for taking a chance on a new author and the time to teach the process.

My churches: Belmont, Nine Mile, and Christ Church

My fellow students, colleagues, and friends.

For all of my life there has always been God even when I didn't know it and couldn't see God. God has pushed me, pulled me, kicked me, lifted me, held me, picked me up, dusted me off, and continually redeemed me and my life. There is always grace, thank God!

Table of Contents

Foreword

My family and I came to Christ Church United Methodist Church just a few weeks before Shauna was to arrive. We were a little timid about a woman pastor. And a karate instructor to boot!

After the summer, when the small group Bible studies were commencing, my wife decided to take Shauna's class - the same class in which this book was developed - and she loved it. Shauna's book was handed to me to read and I enjoyed it as well. I am not one for devotional 'fluff' as I call it, but Shauna's book was different. It will be different. While only one book can really change the world, Shauna's, like that one, is one born out of experience and one which engages the future. Her writing encourages its reader to grow out from the position of a victim and into the position of an empowered Christian who can endure what life throws at them. The book, which you have in your hands, will be one which you can use to engage others who have gone through the experiences that are contained herein. Shauna draws a parallel between Christianity and Karate, and with that, gives you a way to defend yourself, change your attitude, let the past go, and continue on into a bright walk with God. *Victim No More* teaches us that even though life can be hard and we can go through unimaginable pain, we do not have to take the role of a defeated victim!

We have come to know Shauna as one who is filled with a heart of compassion to all. She is teaching us all about moving on, about standing strong, and about being a child of God. I never worried about my son having an archetype to look up to. I did my daughter — my daughters now — as in our previous congregational life, it is truly a man's world. Shauna is providing for us, for our daughters, and others, someone to look up to. Someone who is accepting of others, understands their needs, hurts and worries, and has a great desire to help. This book carries Shauna's personality, her strength, and her humor and across the distance, allows her and her ministry to impact others where they are.

I don't know anything about karate — unless you count all those movies in the 80's — but I do know that the Christian is constantly being called to change masters. Let Shauna tell you how to prevent that. Take these words and incorporate them into your Christian walk. From this book, learn to change an experience that could knock you down into something that lifts you up and makes you stronger. Life can be a fight sometimes, but with the right attitude, we can make it through anything.

I hope that you enjoy this book as both my wife and I did, as I know others have and will! Shauna will be a leader in the Church Universal, and my entire family is happy to have known her.

Joel Watts
Unsettled Christianity
thechurchofjesuschrist.us

INTRODUCTION

As a United Methodist minister who is also a black belt in Shota Kahn karate I am often asked how I can be both a martial artist and a pastor. There have been a lot of jokes about how I will force people to the altar or smack people who get out of line. Then there is always the joke about no one wanting to disobey me in the church because I know how to hurt them! In reality, anyone who is a true martial artist and/or has a deep understanding of the martial arts knows that it is not about violence — it is about mercy, self-discipline, a lot of routine practice, and a whole host of other characteristics that I would like to address.

The martial arts lifestyle is very similar to the Christian lifestyle in many ways. A person who is a true Christian and/or has a deep understanding of Christianity knows that Christianity is about mercy, self-discipline, a lot of routine practice, and a whole host of other characteristics.

While my story is not new to the world, my journey has been different enough to warrant telling about. Within the pages of this book are the lessons I learned that empowered me to turn my life around. I was stuck in a pattern of choosing abusive men and seeing myself as incapable and worthless. I had allowed myself to become powerless and to be constantly controlled, manipulated, and put down. Once I began to realize my pattern and to fight back, my life changed. I went from being the wife of an abusive, manipulative man to being a beaten down single mom, to being inducted into the International Black Belt Hall of Fame. Today I am a UMC minister and a second degree black belt. Today I travel around and tell my story hoping that it will inspire someone else to fight to change their life. I hope that by sharing my insights, realizations, and lessons learned with others, someone will realize their worth and ability and not be afraid to change their life and their world.

SELF-DEFENSE 101

There are some basic rules to self-defense that must be addressed regularly. First and foremost, if it is a place that makes you uncomfortable, do not go there. Avoid places that are not safe, for example, the dark alley, the deserted parking lot, and the neighborhood rough house. It is often difficult to do because we tend to live life assuming that we are perfectly safe. Due to this assumption, we fail to plan ahead. Park in a well-lit area, stay in a group of people, ask to be escorted, and if possible, just don't go after dark to certain areas of town. Most of the time, we have placed ourselves in a dangerous situation simply because we did not notice the danger due to our busy schedules, self-absorption, and unawareness.

We tend to exercise the same lack of awareness in our spiritual lives as well. Too often we go where we should not. We go at the wrong time and we fail to plan ahead. Self-awareness and situational awareness are crucial to the safety of our lives and our souls.

The rule that most folks do not like to hear is that we must always tell someone where we are going, how long we are going to be there, and what route we are taking. The Buddy System is highly recommended for safety and security. In this day and age of cell phones, there is no excuse for your whereabouts not to be known — unless you are doing something you are ashamed of. If that is the case, quit it! It is too easy to live life in a void and then wonder what happened and why no one can find us. Always let someone know your schedule and your whereabouts even if it is a spontaneous stop for ice cream after work. Vary your schedule and your routes as often as possible so that you do not become predictable to a predator. Most predators and attackers are people we know. That is why it is important to tell more than one person and to alternate what we do.

In our spiritual lives, we must also tell people where we are. Too often, we hold on to and keep silent about worries, doubts, faith crises, and problems. We stumble through life unaware that we are all too familiar with our predators and without help we might lose the encounter. We must be aware of our surroundings: what is around us, who is around us, what have we walked into, and where is the exit. We also need to be aware of what is going on in our world. There are always events taking place around us in our communities, world, and lives. As we take note of what is happening around us we need to spend time becoming aware of how we feel and what we think about what is happening. Too little time is spent in self-reflection. Without self-reflection, it is too easy for us to become mindless cattle moving single file toward the same destination with the only view being the rear end of the cow in front of us!

We also go alone too often in our daily lives. It is not that horrible of an inconvenience to wait and include someone else. There is safety in numbers. The added benefit is that company is often nice and a relationship can grow.

This is why church is so important. We were not designed to live life alone. We need to have relationships and interactions in order to grow and change. We need to have companions simply for the added protection.

We also need to remember that in life we are never truly alone. We tend to leave God in the church or somewhere in heaven and we live life as if God is not with us when in fact God is present in our day to day lives. Do not try to be so alone that you become an easy target or the straggling weakling.

When the time comes to be alone, planning ahead is crucial. We need to have quiet time apart from the cares of the world but we need to ensure that it is in a safe place and at a safe time.

Lesson One Exercises

EXERCISE ONE:

A) Just as we defend our persons, we must defend our ability to experience spirituality throughout our days and our lifetime. The same rules apply:
   1) Don't go someplace where it will be robbed from you
   2) Be aware of what is around and what it might mean
   3) Tell someone where you are in life and in your spirit
   4) Plan ahead.
B) What is spirituality?

C) Make a list of places where you feel your spirituality slipping away:

D) Make a list of times when you have not felt spiritual (when you could not feel God or were not aware of God's presence in your life).

E) Make a list of people who consistently and habitually rob you of your ability to feel "spiritual":

F) Make a list of places where you feel restored:

G) Make a list of people who help you become restored:

H) Is there a difference between religion and spirituality? Can someone be spiritual without claiming a certain religion? Can someone be religious and not be spiritual? Offer explanations and thoughts.

I) Where are you in your spiritual journey?

Wondering if God
even exists

Actively seeking the
divine

Have a close personal
relationship

J) What do you need to plan to do to restore your joy or to raise your spiritual awareness?

K) How will you make sure you do what you need to do?

EXERCISE TWO:

A) Read and discuss the following verses:
   Deuteronomy 10:12

   Hosea 6:6

   Micah 6:8

   Ecclesiastes 12:13

   Mark 12:33

   Romans 13:10

   James 1:27

   1) How is true spirituality defined in these scriptures?

   2) Does this change your view of religion/spirituality?

3) Of the traits listed, which do you see in your own spiritual life?

4) Growing edges are the areas in our lives in which we struggle. These are areas that are not quite "right" and we need to apply grace. Growing edges are the traits and characteristics we have that we might try to hide, deny, or ignore. Which do you have that are growing edges?

5) Which traits do you see exhibited by your church?

6) Which are growing edges?

B) Read and discuss the following:
   John 8:24

John 6:53

John 4:24

John 3:5

Luke 13:2, 3

Matthew 5:20

Matthew 18:3

1) What are the spiritual requirements listed in each of these verses that need to be apparent in our lives?

2) Which of these requirements do you see within yourself?

3) Which of these requirements are growing edges for you?

4) Which of these spiritual requirements does your church exhibit?

5) Which of these requirements are growing edges for your church?

CHOOSING OUR ATTITUDE

A) WE ALL HAVE AN ATTITUDE; WHAT'S YOURS?

Key Concept: Decide what your attitude will be.

One of the biggest hurdles that has to be jumped in the martial arts world and in Christianity is attitude. We live with a defeatist attitude that pervades all we do, all we think, and all we say. We just assume that the worst is going to happen and that we will fail before we have even tried to succeed. We raise our children in such a way that they believe that they can do anything and be anybody they choose. Then real life hits, and after a string of rejections and disappointments, there is bitterness and cynicism. This becomes the prevailing attitude for many adults. They assume failure and assume that life will be unfair and there is no way they can achieve what they want to achieve. We desperately need to change how we think about life circumstances and our supposed failures.

I hate the old saying that is used supposedly to encourage someone when they are going through a rough time. You may have heard it: "Sometimes God puts you flat on your back so there is nowhere else to look but up." Did I mention that I really abhor that statement? "Why?" you ask. In the world of martial arts it is accepted in some styles that being flat on your back is one of your most defensible positions. It sounds crazy but think about it a minute. While I freely admit that being flat on my back in a fight is a position I avoid at all costs, I know to instantly do one thing when I have been knocked down: put my feet up.

Let's get a visual picture of what happens in this situation. You are minding your own business one day when suddenly you find yourself knocked down and realize you are being attacked. So, you quickly put your legs up and start pumping like crazy! Soon your attacker gives up (hopefully!). This is why the attacker gives up: when you are flat on your back with your feet up, your legs are longer than anyone's arms are going to be. So, put your legs up and start kicking like a mad person! Kick indiscriminately – there are several areas to choose from in that position. The attacker's groin area is right about where your feet are making that an accessible target. Since they are bent over kicking them in their abdomen and chest is also easy to do. Then if they try to grab you, keep kicking because now they have obligingly put their face in the way of your indiscriminately kicking feet!

I am a firm believer that we need to change how we look at the bad situations in our lives. Instead of bemoaning our fate and waiting to die a horrible death, instead of assuming that God has done this to us for some dark unknown (or known) transgression, we have to look for the opportunity. Instead of assuming that God hates us, is punishing us, is torturing us just because God can, we have to look for the opportunity. Instead of assuming that we are flat on our back and helpless, we have to look for the opportunities. What opportunities?!

I know when we are in the middle of a crisis we think there is nothing good. Then it is a downhill spiral where the more stressed we become the more negative we become until we reach the point where we are angry because the sun rose that morning! We are fairly certain that the sun will explode that day, the sky will fall, or our coffee cup will spring a leak! Stop, take a breath, look again; there are opportunities to be found. Sometimes it requires a little effort but they can be found. The biggest opportunity there is will be the moment that God gives us in which we can learn to trust God. When we do not allow that opportunity to be found we miss God; not because God was not there but because we were not open to receiving what God had to offer. If we allow God the opportunity we will be able to see that God will not let us down. In Hebrews 13:5, we are told by God, "I will never leave you nor forsake you." Now many of us, in response to this, can't wait to start listing off all the moments in our lives when we have felt alone and let down by God. We are always in a hurry to paint God out as a big, bad God who sits in heaven waiting to squash us like bugs the minute we do one little thing wrong! My question to you is this: "Who actually left?" If you are honest with yourself, you will see that you turned your back on God and walked away, most likely so you could pout about something that did not go your way. Come on, admit it, ... you pouted a little bit. At least to the point where you got a good grump on, right?

Well, my friend, while you are off pouting, being angry, running away, and avoiding God, God is patiently waiting for you to turn around so you can get a great big God Hug! Unlike humanity, God loves with no conditions and no strings attached. How good you are does not determine how much God loves you. God just loves you. All God wants in return is you, right now, the way you are. The bad circumstances in your life do not exist merely because God hates you, doesn't notice you, has forgotten you, or just wants to cause you some grief. They just are because we live in a natural world and bad things happen. When humanity first sinned, the pattern was set and creation was no longer perfect. Because of this imperfection bad things happen to good people and to bad people. The problems in your life may not be a direct result of sin in your life, but odds are they are the result of the sins of someone in your life. Folks, let go of the idea that there are problems in your life and terrible situations because you are a horrible person. You may have done some terrible things, you may have suffered terrible things but God loves you anyway. In Romans chapter 8, we are told that nothing can separate us from the love of God (Romans 8:35). Did you catch that? Nothing, *nothing* can separate us from the love of God. The terrible things we suffer do not happen because God does not love us. They happen because they happen. If you have done something to bring it on yourself, you know why it happened. If someone else did something, you know why that situation is happening. But sometimes, bad things just happen. Sometimes there is no reason, no explanation, and no consolation to be found.

Rest assured; God loves you. Just put your feet up. You are now in your most defensible position for the fight of your life.

In order to further define this perspective, let's consider how much He has invested in the human race already. We exist, a plan for salvation has been made, we continue to exist and accomplish amazing ministries! God has invested in each of us and does not want us to fail. God does not want us to be victims. God does not want us to be survivors. God wants us to be conquerors.

Unfortunately, the one who gets the blame is God. The prevailing attitude is one of accusation toward God because the dreams, aspirations, plans, and desires have not come to fruition and there must be someone to blame. We, as a society, have lost the fine art of being responsible for our actions. We seldom can just admit what we have done wrong. Instead we supply people with a long list of reasons to justify the transgression.

It is exceedingly difficult for us to stay dedicated to an action or a dream in which we do not receive instant gratification. In a world in which we can have food, money, clothing, toys, tools, and anything else we can think of instantly, we have lost the fine art of waiting and holding true to a course of action to the end. We have to learn to hold steady, to wait, and be patient in yielding results.

Karate class is inherently one of the most boring times during the week. We do the same things, in the same order, and most of the time we see the same faces. I know that class will start a few minutes late because we all catch up on the news of the week. The same people will come in late. The same people will forget the same needed items for class and they will be magically produced. We will warm up with stretches and exercises before we practice our basic movements. After basic movements, we will run drills and practice self-defense moves. Next in the sequence is kata practice. Katas are forms that link all basic movements into a routine. For the style of karate that I practice, there are three basic stances, blocks, and kicks. Throw in some closed-fist and open-handed hits along with a few showy moves and you have a kata.

It takes a lot of classes and a lot of practice before there is any sense of accomplishment. The first few weeks, new students leave class with their heads spinning due to all the new information. Learning to move their bodies in new ways makes them awkward and self-conscious. This awkwardness does not just go away. It takes time. For some people it takes a lot of time. A large percentage of people realize they are not going to be Bruce Lee in three weeks and they leave. Some hang on and rank up two or three belts. Most quit by the time they reach the half-way mark. My instructor has always told me that only one person out of every hundred people make it to black belt. A large percentage of people quit after they have attained their black belt. For some reason, many people view the black belt as the end, the goal, the symbol of accomplishment. In reality, becoming a black belt means that that student has just become a *serious* student. All the study, practice, and time up to that point are just so that student can now become a truly serious and committed student.

Now the real work begins. This work is the work of perfection. The day a student gets their black belt is a great day. They have a special moment with the Grand Master, they get their black belt, and they take their vows and receive words of wisdom from the Grand Master. This wisdom usually consists of a reminder of who we are and the responsibility we have in caring for those around us. All the black belts shake their hand and congratulate them. All the students present from all over the area come and shake their hands and congratulate them. They go out to eat afterward and have a celebration. Sometimes there are gifts and cards and big to-dos with family and friends.

Then, they wake up the next morning and find that they are so sore they can hardly move. They find all the noogies, bruises, cuts, and broken toes that they were on too much of an adrenaline high to notice the day before. Over the next three days they gradually work through all the soreness and are just starting to move normally again and then it is time for the first "black belts only" class.

They walk into class managing to strut despite any broken toes and residual muscle soreness and take their place in the line-up. There is warm-up with stretches and exercises. The routine is familiar so they are confident that this class will be a piece of cake. Then comes the practice of the basic movements. This is the point at which the new black belt is thinking that they have this down. They have been doing basic movements one to three times a week for the last six to eight years. They jump into the drills with gusto assuming that there will be nothing different. Then the highest ranking black belt present will pull out a yard stick. This yard stick is taken to each student and each leg, each arm, each big toe, and each fist, and each chin is measured for the distance and the angle. The perfecting work has begun. The first time in the class is humbling. To realize that the requirements have been learned but are not perfect and to realize that perfection is required is humbling and inspiring.

When we have an encounter with God and realize that redemption and salvation can be provided, we are on a spiritual high. We have had a conversion experience or a new realization of who God is and what God can do in our lives. We have had the realization that we are truly free and that God is in control. We have been to a wonderful retreat or seminar and we are on the mountain. We have had a worship experience that inspired us to new heights. Whatever the occasion or the experience we suddenly feel powerful and close to God. We feel like we can do no wrong and the world will just naturally understand this experience and go along with us.

Then we go back to our regular routine, our ordinary lives, and our predictable ruts. Almost overnight we lose the energy and the joy. We find ourselves questioning God and the experience that we had. We have to take the attitude of the highest ranking black belt and pull out the yard stick. We have to measure each angle and length in our lives to see if we are in the proper alignment to carry on and do the work and live the life that God would have us live. We are being perfected in those moments. We have to be ready for a really good challenge by relaxing and letting God do the perfecting. We resist change. We really resist the long, hard, and involved work of getting to the change. It goes against our nature to be the

Christians that God calls us to be. We want to stick with our safe and normal routine so we can feel like we have accomplished the task of fulfilling our Christian duties but not really be invested in them. We forget that when we experience God and choose God that now we are truly committed students of God. We are to practice God, study the word of God, be invested in the people of God, draw people to God, and be willing to be perfected by God.

There is another old saying about how anything worth having is worth working for. In our current society of instant gratification, we have forgotten how to set ourselves to keep at it until we have accomplished our goal. The minute it gets hard or circumstances stop going our way, we take it personally and quit. Every dream can be accomplished. It just takes more work than dreaming to accomplish the goal.

Years ago, I was married to a man who did not let me dream. He was controlling and could be harsh and cruel. I still struggle with the ideas that he planted in my head about how I could not do anything right and there was something wrong with me. Often my first reaction to anything was to assume that I would not be able to do it before I even tried.

That time in my life is a time that I don't often provide details for. It took a long time for me to admit what had happened to me. Being verbally, mentally, and emotionally abused is a terrible way to live life. People, men and women, who live that way are beat down in such a way that many never rise above and recover. Many do not even realize what is happening to them. Most of the time, by the time it is realized, the pattern has been established and the assumption is made that it is too late. It is never too late to recover yourself. It is never too late to stop the cycle and to rise above. It is never too late to have a situation, a life, or a person be redeemed by the loving grace of God.

For me, the rise above it all started with my son's karate teacher. She saw in me the mousiness, the lack of self-esteem and self-confidence. She recognized the pattern of my life and knew what was happening; however, she also saw in me the potential to be more and to do more. She started to teach me karate too. Before long, I was a steady student and began to thrive. My personality began to assert itself and I began to realize what was happening to me. Needless to say this caused some extreme misery for my husband as he realized that he was losing control. The situation escalated as I was changing. He began to realize that I was going to rise above regardless of his repeated attempts to keep me beaten down.

It is a freeing moment in life to begin to think for yourself and do for yourself. It is empowering to realize that God does not beat us down and keep us under a big thumb.

Unfortunately, that marriage ended in divorce. In hindsight, I believe that it was God saving my life and putting me back where I was supposed to be. I would not be where I am today if I was still married to him. I do not know if I would even still be alive. I had reached the point where I prayed one of us would die and I did not care which one of us it was. I just wanted the misery to end. I was not loved; I was being destroyed. I was not cared for, I was controlled. I was not allowed to be happy because he wasn't happy. It took a lot of counseling to get past the damage that had been done. It took a lot of time to realize that there was another way to have a healthy relationship.

Sometimes, what seems to be horrible life circumstances is, in reality, God saving your life and your soul. When we stray off God's plan for our lives, God can and often will intervene to provide us the choice to return to that plan. So often our pain is a result of our own poor choices. But that pain can and will end. Nothing in this world lasts forever.

Today, I am a black belt in karate. I was inducted into the International Blackbelt Hall of Fame in Pittsburgh in 2006 as Woman of the Year. My Soke (grandmaster) heard my story and shared this story as a way to inspire others. Today I am a United Methodist minister and I am married to someone who empowers me and encourages me to try new things, to go new places, and to be the best person I can be. Today, I work with people who have been abused and need to learn that they are worth the fight to change their lives. Today, I travel around and tell people my story and use karate techniques to demonstrate how we can be empowered by changing our attitudes, our mindsets, and our habits.

Did I do this on my own? No. We sell ourselves short too often. We forget that as children of God we have at our disposal unlimited power and promise. We have to stop thinking human and small and start thinking like we have an awesome God.

B) LETTING GO

Key Concept: Leave it at the gym.

Before and after each class we have a bowing in ceremony. This consists of much bowing, reciting the karate creed, in my class prayer, and a time of meditation. This is especially important at the end of class. During class, there can be tension as a new technique is struggled with, sparring takes place, tempers flare, or frustration grows. The time of meditation at the end of class is a time to breathe, focus, and let it go. Whatever was upsetting, difficult, or frustrating is left on the floor of the gym while we walk away. We do not take it with us.

In our Christian lives there are events that frustrate us, anger us, and hurt us. This makes our prayer time all the more important. We have to leave what we take to the throne of grace *at* the throne of grace. We do not pick it back up and take it with us. It is done, it is over, and the problems are in the hands of Someone who is better able to handle them. God really does not need our help in that regard. What we are to take with us is the peace, joy, and hope that we are offered in return. The help we are to offer is to share these gifts with those around us and bring more people to that throne of grace.

Practice and study is in order to form good habits so that when a fight is in order you are able to fight well. Stay balanced and focused on the word of God and the things of God. In Philippians

4:6-8, we are told to think about things that are good, holy, right, noble, etc. We are not to focus on the things that tear us away from God, bring us to despair, or make us act in a way that God would not have us act.

It is too easy to focus only on the negative but that tendency must be fought. The only way to defeat that habit is to change what we focus on and think about. We forget that we really do have a choice in these matters. Focus. Breathe. Bend your knees. Learn from your mistakes. Let God take control.

At the end of every fight, we shake hands, bow to each other, and bow to the sensei who was officiating the fight. At the end of this book, I will bow to you and shake your hand. It is difficult to know when to fight, when to breathe, when to let go, and when to walk away. In life there are no easy answers, no quick solutions, and no quick comebacks. There is a lot of work, a lot of struggle and a lot of uncertainty. In the end, all we can come out with is the knowledge of who we are and where we are going. We may never find all the answers and we may never be truly at peace with ourselves. We may never understand the world, the people in it, or the ways of God. What we will know is who *we* are in God. We can know what our purpose is through God and we can know the peace provided by God.

Know this: you are loved; you can be forgiven; God has a purpose for you. Your presence on this planet has been noticed, your absence will be noticed as well. You are needed and important to this world to spread a message of hope. You can have a new beginning and you can teach someone else how to have a new beginning.

When I first stood across the line from someone to spar, I got into my fighting stance, looked at them and ran for the bathroom to lose my dinner. Ran back to the line, repeated the process one more time and then finally, I fought.

That said, keep your chin up. Keep your hands up and your elbows tucked. Stay on your toes; keep circling, breathing, and stay focused. Keep your knees bent and your back straight. What we seldom realize is that most of time the joy is not in the victory, but in the fight itself.

Lesson Two Exercises

EXERCISE ONE:

1) On the graph paper following this page make a plot of your lifetime. Start with the day you were born and start plotting points that represent any major events in your life. Use the entire graph paper so that there is an extreme difference in the highs and the lows. Label each point so that you know what it is.
2) Now connect the dots so that the time line is visible.
3) Now turn the paper upside down. Suddenly our lows become our highs and our highs become our lows.
4) Go back to each low point (now a high point) and write beside it what you learned about God during that time.
5) Discuss in your small groups the following:
   What was your primary emotion during that time in your life? What is your primary emotion *now* as you remember that time in your life? How has your attitude changed? How did you experience God then? How do you experience God *now* as you remember that time?

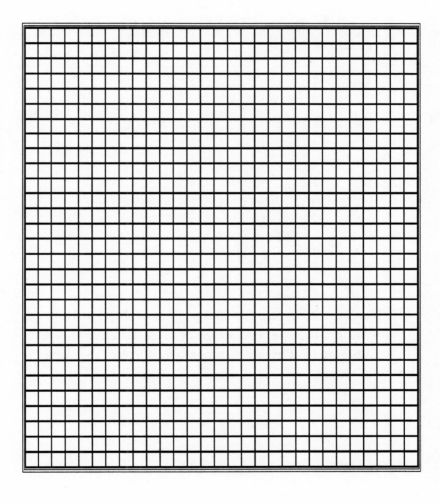

EXERCISE TWO:

A) Read and discuss the following scriptures:
   Isaiah 61:3

   Jeremiah 30:19

   Jeremiah 31:13

   Hosea 2:15

   John 16:20

B) How will the promise restoration be fulfilled in our lives?

C) The ways in which God restores us include deliverance, provision of hope, and the vision of a risen Savior. Which of these acts of restoration need to take place in your life?

1) If it is deliverance, what do you need to be delivered from (for example: anger, an unforgiving heart, bitterness, apathy, circumstances, etc)?

2) If you need to be delivered from circumstances, what has been your role in these circumstances?

3) If your hope needs to be restored, what happened in your life that resulted in a loss of hope?

4) If you need a vision of a risen Savior, what has happened in your life that has resulted in the loss of seeing Christ in your life?

EXERCISE THREE:

A large percentage of women who are attacked were chosen by the attacker because they had a pony tail. A pony tail provides the attacker with a handle that gives them control over the victim's entire body. Wherever the attacker pulls the head, the body must follow. In life, whatever has our head, has all of us. Whatever we spend all our time and energy thinking about, worrying about, fretting over, and consumed with, controls our lives.

A) What do you think about? What consumes the major portion of your thoughts and energy?

    1)   Read Philippians 4:8

    2)   According to Scripture, what should we be thinking about?

    3)   How do we make the conscious decision to not become consumed by thoughts about all that is negative?

    4)   Does this mean that we can never think about anything that is bad, negative, harmful, etc.?

B) Read Psalm 136

    1)   What is the constantly repeating refrain?

2) When we look at our society and what we are surrounded by, it becomes apparent that we are consistently and constantly being put down. According to society, most of us have some sort of serious flaw that makes us unacceptable or unlovable. We are too young, too old, too fat, too thin, too poor, too stupid, etc. Anytime we encounter our society, it is easy to come away feeling inadequate. In a person to person relationship in which this occurs, it would be classified as an abusive relationship. The mental, emotional, and verbal abuse that each of us receives due to the society in which we live is staggering and we pay a heavy price. There are catch phrases that people who are in abusive relationships use repeatedly. These phrases are not in response to an unusually long, hard day. These phrases are said several times a day regardless of health and/or circumstance. These phrases include, "I'm tired," "I feel old," "I just can't do anything right," "Nothing good ever happens to me," "I should have expected that anything I did would fail," etc. Their constant refrain indicates where they are in life, where they are in spirit, and how they feel about themselves. More people than ever say those refrains who are not in any other abusive relationship except the one they share with society. Take a few moments to consider and discuss what the constantly repeating refrain is in your life. What is that refrain?

3) What has been your experience in our society? Have you been made to feel inadequate? What was said or done (blatant or subliminally) that has made you feel that way? Examples include always skinny women and muscular men as models, women attacked in movies and always being completely helpless (even when their hands and feet are free), blond jokes, ugly jokes, etc.

4) What/who does God say you are and what you are capable of? See Philippians 4:13, Psalm 139:14, and Romans 8:37.

5) If the refrain in your life is negative, how can it be changed?

6) Go back to the life-graph and write beside each high point (a former low point) which of God's promises was fulfilled during that time. How many of those low points became the highest points of your life? Why do you see them as high points now?

7) Celebrate your high points (the original ones!) by sharing those moments with each other.

8) Write a Psalm of your own using that constantly repeating refrain. If the refrain in your life is negative, for example, "If something bad is going to happen it is going to happen to me," use the *opposite* thought in the refrain, "If something *good* is going to happen, it is going to happen to *me*."

WHO DO YOU SERVE?

A) WHO'S YOUR MASTER, NOW?

Key Concept: Know who you are and who you serve.

In the martial arts world that I happen to live in, it is often a fairly simple identification process when watching a student to know who their master instructor is. The traits of that master are evident in the style and the manner in which that student performs their katas. Sometimes, an instructor might even add to a kata by putting in their signature move. This signature move is the move by which that instructor is known in some way. They have perfected it and are known for it and the fact that no one does it as well as they do or in the unique manner in which they do it.

Another way to identify a student's master is to listen to their kya. In karate we have a yell that we refer to as the kya. This kya can be any noise so long as it shows spirit and intimidates the opponent. Some master instructors have all the students who study under them yell their names. So at tournaments and tests there are all kinds of names being yelled all day long.

My husband, Wayne, and I teach at our own dojo. Some of the students might yell "Wayne" and some might yell "Shauna." I kept my maiden name so my husband and I have different last names. His last name is Hollandsworth and mine is Hyde. One day in class we were all playing around and we started putting our last names together in different combinations until we found one we liked. The younger children especially started laughing when the combination HyHo was selected. Now the dojo kya for the HyHo Dojo is "HyHo." While I find it quite funny and the students find it enjoyable, my poor husband just stands and shakes his head muttering something about dwarfs and apples ....

In the Christian world that all Christians should be living in, it should be apparent who our master is. We should act like our master, move like our master, and have the "signature move" of our master. The signature move for Christians is love.

First, in Matthew 22:37-39 we are taught that we are to love others as we love ourselves. Second, in the same passage we are taught to love God with our heart, our soul, and our minds. Jesus tells us repeatedly in the Gospels that we are to love our enemies and forgive those who persecute us (Matthew 5:44, Mark 12:33, Luke 6:35).

This line of thought clashes with the society we live in. We live in a world in which we are taught to look out for number one. We are encouraged to get revenge, to have our say, and to tell people off. We are not encouraged to speak softly (Proverbs 15:1) in answer to anger and accusation. We are not encouraged to show mercy and forgiveness. A true Christian seeking a genuine relationship with God should and will turn to the Scriptures in difficult situations for answers such as:

Matthew 5:7, "Blessed are the merciful."

Luke 6:36, "Be merciful, just as your Father is merciful."

1 Peter 1:3, "in his great mercy ...."

Altogether there are at least 50 scripture references in which God is described as being a merciful God or Christians are being reminded to show mercy. In order to show mercy, we must learn to love that person for who they are in that moment. We are not all lovable all the time.

I have heard many a preacher and teacher talk about how loving others as we love ourselves indicates that we cannot love others until we love ourselves. I am not convinced this is a self-esteem issue. I deal with people every day who hate themselves, yet they are clothed, fed, and always have what they want. It seems as if no matter how much they hate themselves they care for themselves to some extent. When I read, hear, or think of that commandment, I wonder why we cannot "hate" others like we "hate" ourselves.

If we could "hate" our enemy by clothing them and feeding them, we could change lives. If we could "hate" our enemy by listening to them and comforting them, we could change the world. I think this commandment is telling us that we are to love others, care for others, and consider each human life as precious.

A true martial artist understands the concept of mercy. As we go up through the ranks we are taught more powerful techniques. We are taught moves that will maim, seriously hurt, and even kill another person. There is an oath that we are all required to learn and know in our organization:

> I come to you with only karate, my empty hands. I am a law abiding citizen. At no time will I ever use the techniques taught to me in a manner that will inflict personal injury. Nor will I bodily harm anyone except in cases of emergency needs whereby my honor, life, country, or the lives and physical safety of others may depend upon my knowledge and application of these techniques. This is my creed, karate!

There is a certain point where we have to decide what we believe and how we will behave for ourselves. Just because I know how to rip your eyeball out through your nose bone does not mean that when I am angry with you, I have the right or the justification to do it! Just as I am expected to take responsibility for my actions as a black belt, I am also expected to take responsibility for my actions as a Christian. Mercy begins with a decision not to hurt someone in response to them hurting you. Mercy leads to forgiveness and is the beginning of demonstrating grace. Folks, when we know every day that we have the right to become children of God because we have been forgiven, we do not have the right to withhold forgiveness from others. The only way for others to come to know and understand the mercy and forgiveness of God is to demonstrate that mercy and forgiveness ourselves.

Now, I am not telling you to be blind to what others do; I am saying that we need to show mercy. Forgiving someone is what is required of us. If they have decimated our trust and have a proven track record of bad choices, spitefulness, cruelty, etc. it is okay not to trust them. If they choose to change and prove to us that they have changed, then they can earn back the trust. What is required of us is that we show mercy and forgive. Forgiving is not easy and often the work of forgiveness is left out of the conversation. The act of forgiveness can take a lifetime of moment by moment choices and we repeatedly choose to forgive them just as God forgives us. When we are too angry or bitter or hurt to even begin to think about forgiveness then we do the slow work of getting ready to forgive. The act of forgiveness requires the inclusion of God. Most of the time humans simply cannot completely forgive on our own. What I have discovered is that over time if we do not give up but continuously choose to forgive, eventually we forgive the person(s) and ourselves in the process. Doing the work is the important part. Understanding that forgiveness, as a general rule, does not just happen immediately all the time, is the key to developing a forgiving spirit.

Once we become a black belt in my organization, we are ranked based upon the quality of students that we produce and the level of commitment that we demonstrate. We are expected to teach correct technique and the correct attitude of showing and demonstrating mercy at all times. If we do not teach correct technique, the lives of our students are at stake. If we do not teach the correct attitude, the lives of those who set themselves up as opponents to our students are at stake. Either way, the responsibility falls to the teacher. Just as correct technique is not an option neither is showing mercy an option – both must simply be done, period.

The style of our art is quick and brutal. In three moves or less, we are to have our opponent down and are to be *leaving*. We are not to stay around and finish the job, go in for the kill, or even get in a few vicious kicks for the sake of posterity. We are only to defend ourselves and leave.

God also defended the world in three moves or less. Jesus was born, Jesus was crucified, and Jesus rose again. This is a master who will not enslave us but will empower us. This is a master who has taught what we needed to know so that our lives may be changed and even saved. This master has taught us by example what is required of us.

Our lives should reflect who our master is. It should not be a shock to friends, neighbors, and co-workers that we are Christians. Any jokes such as, "Wow, I thought football (insert whatever is appropriate here, this is just an example) was your God" is an indicator that we are not succeeding in showing who our master is. More than that, we are not succeeding in knowing who our master is for ourselves.

Knowing who our master is also requires knowing our master. Any relationship that we want, we tend to invest in. If there is someone we want to date, we hover and find excuses to talk to them. We spend hours talking about senseless topics on the phone. We wake up thinking about them and go to bed thinking about them. We get that silly smile on our faces when we see them and we feel giddy when they smile back. The relationships that last are the relationships in which both people were committed to finding time to be together. Years later, they can still talk for hours on the phone and leave each other silly notes.

Our relationship with God requires the same kind of commitment. We have to seek out time to talk with God even about senseless topics. We have to sit and enjoy the gifts that God leaves for us in the form of sunsets, sunrises, morning mist, flowers, and children's laughter. We also have to take the time to listen to God in return. Just be silent every so often. Turn everything off and be silent. In the martial arts, we call this meditation. We are silent and yet focused. We listen to what is around us and we listen to the silence. In this silence we can begin to know our master and come know the voice of the master.

One of the characteristics that I recognize instantly about my sensei is her voice. I can be in the middle of a fight in a gym with eight other fights going on and I can still hear her voice screaming instructions to me from clear across that gym! It is a voice that I have learned to obey without question, without argument, and without attitude. It is a voice that I have learned will never bring me harm or lead me to take the wrong action. Knowing this voice and trusting the voice is about respect and trust that have become a choice to obey. This is a relationship in which the trust has been learned and earned. This is a relationship of knowing that obedience to that voice will help me in the middle of a fight. This is a relationship in which I have learned that the orders issued by that voice are for my safety, improvement, and eventual victory.

As Christians, we need to be able to hear and recognize the voice of our master. This is a voice that will never lead us astray. This is the one voice in our lives that will never hurt us, get us in trouble, lead us in the wrong direction, or jeopardize our safety. This is a voice that will lead us into a relationship that will be about a trust that is learned and earned. This trust has to be developed so that instant obedience is a choice that is instinctual to us; however, we can never know this voice unless we make time to hear it. We have to be silent and focus on God so that we become familiar with the voice of our Master.

When we decide that our Master is God, we change. I tell women in seminars that Paris Hilton does not have anything on us! We are daughters of the One True and Living God. We are the crown princesses to the Royal Kingdom of Heaven. We can become anything and anyone we want to be. We can be terrific wives, daughters, sisters, and friends. We can have good jobs and wonderful children. We may not be able to have it all but we can have it all IN CHRIST. There is no habit that we cannot break, no wrong that cannot be righted, no dream that cannot be realized, and no goal that cannot be achieved.

Men, do you know who you are? You are the adopted sons of God. You are members of a "royal priesthood" (1 Peter 2:9). You can be terrific fathers, husbands, sons, brothers, and friends. You can have a good job and a terrific family. You may not be able to have it all but you can have it all IN CHRIST. There is no habit that we cannot break, no wrong that cannot be righted, no dream that cannot be realized, and no goal that cannot be achieved.

Don't forget who you are. When you are solid in this knowledge you are solid in the knowledge of who your Master is. This is a Master who created us to be joyful and creative; a Master who wants us to be fulfilled and complete and a Master who knows us and loves us anyway!

When we choose God to be our master, we are not relinquishing our freedom. We do not give up our free will, we do not have to give up the essence of who we are and what we want. God is a master who will empower us to realize our dreams. Our dreams may change as we get in tune with that voice, but that is still our choice. A true master will always be a master who is not threatened by who you are and what you can accomplish. A true master will not hold back their students. A true master sees the potential and guides the student in such a way as to realize that potential.

B) OUS, SENSEI

Key Concept: Respect

So, now you are wondering what Wonderland or Walgreen's World I happen to live in, right? I admit it is hard work not to be angry and retaliate. To let people's garbage go in the garbage can instead of in us is a constant job. I have failed many times and for many years. There are still people in my life that cause me to bristle just at the mention of their names. These are people that I can lie awake at night dreaming of things to do to make their lives miserable. But, again, it comes down to a waste of time and energy and ability to prevent them from having control over us.

Remember those two commandments from Jesus (love God with all your heart, soul and mind and love your neighbor as yourself)? It all boils down to respect. We forget that respecting others and loving others is a conscious choice we make on a daily basis.

In karate, there is a lot a bowing. I tell my students, "When in doubt, bow!" You can never go wrong by showing respect to the other person.

It is easy to forget that we are all human and we all hurt. We can get so focused on our own pain that all we do is take it out on those around us. The waitress who screwed up the lunch order may have been a single mom with three children and bills she can't pay. That morning, one of her children woke up sick. She can't call off so all she can do is go to work and worry about what is happening at home. However, most of her customers will only see that she made a mistake. Most of her customers will yell at her, mistreat her, not leave a tip, or complain to the manager.

The person who cut you off in traffic may have been a grandfather who has had to take on the raising of his grandchildren and has had to rush to the school for an emergency. The typical reaction from those of us that were cut off will be one of yelling, swearing, and even violence.

It is easier to treat those around us with respect. A kind word instead of a harsh remark, yielding the right of way instead of demanding that we are first are ways in which we can simply show a little respect. This is contrary to how we think and operate today. We have to unlearn what we have learned. What we have learned has become habit and has become integrated into our personalities and behaviors.

When new students start karate class, they struggle so much with all the new information, unlearning what they have learned and breaking the habits they have picked up. They learn to walk differently, stand differently, and move their bodies differently. They learn to use their muscles instead of their joints to lift, turn, spin, and move. All the sloppy habits of movement must be corrected and perfected in order to perform the techniques well. Not doing them correctly or well often results in personal injury.

It is time to step back and relearn some mindsets and behaviors that result in personal injury and injury to those around us.

When I was in Israel, I saw people backing away from the holy places. They had too much respect to turn their backs on the place and walk away. In karate, at tests and tournaments, we are taught and we teach others to never turn their backs on the black belts who are the judges and testers. It is a sign of respect. Turning your back on someone is telling them that they are not worthy of your time and attention. Turning your back means that you are done and are not interested in what they might have to offer. Showing a little respect goes a long way. It could be the difference of a really bad day or a really good day for someone who is desperate just to have one good day.

C) A LITTLE HUMILITY ....

Key Concept: Genuine humility will win every time.

Showing respect and bowing at someone to acknowledge them as superior requires some humility. Obeying a boss, trusting the advice of a parent, or not forcing our opinions onto others all requires a little humility.

The older I get, the harder it is to be corrected. I find that to be true with most people. We get set in our ways and assume that our way is the only right way. When we make that assumption we cease to listen or consider any other ways. Our reaction is to shut down the other person as fast as we can. Sometimes, the other way really is the better way. We have to be humble enough to accept correction. As karate students, our lives could depend on it; as Christians, our souls could depend on it.

All the training in the world won't make a blackbelt. The belt is earned not only after the training but also after proving that humility, mercy, and the willingness to protect others is an integral part of the character of the student. Earning that belt is a wonderful achievement; however, it is the beginning of new responsibilities. Each black belt is required to teach not only karate to other students but also what is required of us later. Any student who cannot exhibit humility, mercy, and kindness is not granted their belt. Any blackbelt who acts dishonorably can be punished.

With the ability and the knowledge comes the responsibility never to harm but always to teach and to show mercy. As Christians, we have all been given the responsibility to tell others that they can also have a new life in Christ. We have received an assignment to go and preach the gospel to the world. Mark 16:15 is where we find this assignment. We live life in such a way that we seem to think that evangelism is only for evangelists; however, preaching the gospel is more than just telling the story of how Jesus came, suffered, died, and rose again for the sins of the world. The gospel is ultimately about love, hope, mercy, and forgiveness.

I have never understood why we sit on the information that those around us need in order to be healed and have hope. As neighbors, co-workers, friends, and relatives, we can have a greater impact than any evangelist in this world. We spend too much time worrying over the details and nitpicking at what it all really means. We have become complacent and content in a world that is dying and needs what we have more than ever. It is not easy to put ourselves in a position in which we can be ridiculed or rejected. We are afraid that we will somehow be hurt or made a fool of. It is easy to forget that Jesus was ridiculed, rejected, and hurt for us. It is easy to become complacent and leave the work to others. It is easy to stay in our ruts and our routines and hope that we are never put in a position in which we have to actually put ourselves out there and accomplish something in the name of God. Just as blackbelts have an obligation to teach others how to protect their lives, Christians have an obligation to teach others how their souls can be saved. By this I do not mean the spiritual abuse (completely separate book!) that is so often applied to force people into salvation. Truly being saved means developing a genuine relationship with God and growing into the amazing person that God knows you can be.

I tell my congregations that I know that somewhere along the way in every day, I am going to do something to make a fool of myself. This has been an inevitable part of my life ever since I can remember. I may as well do it on purpose and get it over with! People may reject the gospel, they may reject us, but a seed is still planted. A seed that will one day take root and grow. We try to complicate the assignment by forgetting that God will do the saving — not us. We spread the seeds and do the work of maintaining and growing the garden. God takes care of the saving, the changing, and the perfecting.

I struggle every day as a pastor knowing that while we spend time debating over the particulars of our faith, there are people dying without hope and without salvation. Too many religious folk spend too much time arguing over whether or not women can be pastors, how and when to baptize, whose theology is the correct theology, which denomination is the best one or the right one, and who has the most accurate interpretation of the Gospel. In the end, it does not and should not matter. We have all been called by God to spread the Gospel and provide people with a message of hope and salvation. I believe in today's world God is calling anyone who will hear and answer the call regardless of gender, race, age, or denominational affiliation. God wants the world to hear that hope and salvation are just a decision away. While we debate senseless and often unimportant issues, souls are being lost. We are failing and it is time to change the tide. We all have a story to tell that reflects hope and salvation. It is time, regardless of who you are, to tell that story.

We need to have the humility to accept all who have been called by God. We need to have the humility to realize that we are all on the same team. We should all have the same goal — spreading the Gospel. We should all have the humility to know that we are not what is needed in this world — it is the message we are to bring to this world. We are not the Savior; Jesus is.

When we become Christians, our lives are no longer about us. A little humility goes a long way in restoring focus in our lives and on our ministries. We are all to become more like Jesus. We are to become Christ-like and Christ-filled. We are to teach others how to obtain the love, mercy, forgiveness, and peace that is offered by our Savior.

We may not all be called to be pastors or missionaries. That's okay! We are all called to spread the gospel and to work for the

Kingdom of Heaven. Sunday School teachers, lay leaders, youth workers, nursery aides, treasurers, greeters, musicians, etc., all play a vital role in putting the message out there. If you have never been asked to play a more active role, volunteer. Your pastor may not be aware of your desires, interests, and abilities. What team or committee could you contribute to? What ideas do you have? What role could you play that would help in spreading the gospel? There is always work to be done; however, the number of willing workers keeps decreasing. No more excuses. No more leaving the work to others because there is a lack interest, commitment, or ability. Where would you be today if God had not taken an interest in you? Where would you be today if Christ had not been committed to His role?

Humility is what is needed, not excuses. We are all to contribute and work on the same team. We are all to do it together as a unified body. There is no one greater than another. This is not a contest. This is not a turf war. This is an assignment that we have to work together in order to succeed. We have to be willing to do tasks we may not want to do, work with people we do not understand, or take a back seat when we want glory. We all have an important role to play in providing hope and salvation to a dying world. That role is clearly laid out in the Bible. We are to love one another, love God, and share the gospel to the world.

Lesson Three Exercises

EXERCISE ONE:

In the martial arts, we have a Master. This Master is the person who teaches us, trains us, recognizes our potential and our weaknesses. This Master cares for us, is our cheerleader, pushes us to do better, get stronger, and teaches us what we need to know to save our lives. Our Master constantly works at perfecting us, encouraging us be all that they know we can be.

A) Read Matthew 6:24 and Luke 16: 1-13.

    1) Who/what do you serve?

    2) How does your life reflect who your Master is?

    3) Read Galatians 5:22 and 6:1-10.

    4) According to these scriptures, what behaviors should be evident in our lives if God is truly our Master?

    5) Which of these behaviors do you consistently exhibit?

6) Which of these behaviors do you continually struggle with?

7) What conflict is in your life because you are trying to serve more than one Master?

8) What other Master are you trying to serve?

9) How can you change or resolve this conflict? What would God have you do?

EXERCISE TWO:

A) Read the following verses and discuss:

Psalm 30:5

Psalm 34:19

Psalm 41:3

Isaiah 43:2

John 14:1, 2

Romans 8:28

2 Corinthians 4:17

2 Corinthians 12:9

1 Peter 4:12, 13

Revelation 21:4

Psalm 37:3

Mark 9:23

Mark 11:24

Luke 17:6

John 3:14, 15

John 6:35

John 12:46

John 14:12

Romans 1:16

Hebrews 13:5

1) List the promises of God described in the verses:

2) How   do   these   promises   influence   your
    thinking/feelings about having God as your Master?

3) Which promises speak most deeply to you?

4) Which promises have you experienced in life?

5) What promises do you need for your life now?

EXERCISE THREE:

A) Consider the Two Great Commandments. What does it mean to you to love others as yourself? Do you love yourself? Do you love others? Do you love someone else even when do you not love yourself? Who is your enemy? When you hate yourself, do you still provide at least minimal care for your physical body? Can you do the same for an enemy?

B) What work of forgiveness do you need to do in your life? How are you working towards forgiving someone? What do you need to do differently?

BEING AWARE

SITUATIONAL AWARENESS ....

Key Concept: Do what it takes to be prepared for anything.

The whole premise behind any martial arts style is preparation. We practice, practice, and practice some more on a regular basis. Then when we think we are done, we practice some more. We study ideas, moves, and katas. We get together and we discuss theories on what we can do to be better, teach better, and what will work the best. There are books are about karate. There are movies and DVD's that can be purchased to learn new katas or a new style. There are seminars, workshops, camps, and tournaments, and tests. There is no excuse for not learning new techniques. There is no excuse for not improving on technique already learned.

We are taught to practice our katas in our minds whenever we have to wait somewhere, or when we need to relax, or whenever we decide to do it. It is a wonderful technique to employ when in a stressful situation such as medical procedure. My sensei told me of a time when she had to have an MRI. She closed her eyes and started going through all the katas she knew. Before she knew it the test was over and she had remained calm through the entire procedure.

We practice so that our bodies and our minds automatically know what to do when an emergency situation arises. The hope is that we have practiced so much that our bodies will just react to the situation even if our brains are in panic mode. Hopefully, we have practiced so much that our brains won't panic either!

We practice so much because we have so many katas we have to know! If we did not practice all of them on a regular basis, we would forget them all.

In the system I am in, once a brown belt level is reached, we are expected to help teach. If regular practice did not take place, you would not remember the katas and the techniques and therefore would not be able to teach them. Once a black belt level is reached, you are graded on the quality of students that you produce. Practice is not only essential; it is absolutely crucial. The amount of practice correlates directly to the quality of technique, speed, accuracy, and quality of instruction. Quality and preparation cannot be achieved without practice.

As Christians, there are books we can read. There is one specific library of books that is particularly essential – the Bible. There are movies and DVD's that can provide education and inspiration. There are seminars, workshops, retreats, and conferences. There are people who get together to discuss theories and ideas. Classes of people get together to learn and grow and to find ways to improve technique. We cannot improve unless we invest in that improvement. We must practice! We must study! We must be open to growth and development.

The real key to practice is attitude. Attitude keeps coming into play, doesn't it? We have to approach it with the desire to do it. If we approach practice halfheartedly, then we learn halfheartedly. If we do not give our all in practice, we are training ourselves to not give our all when we need it. In the art of defending yourself, halfhearted technique will result in your death.

In the art of Christianity, halfhearted technique will result in your spiritual death. It is imperative that we approach church, Bible study (corporate and private) with excitement, the intent to learn and grow, with purpose, and with energy.

Are you one of those people who leave church unhappy and discontented? Do you find fault with the music, the sermon, the way the person sitting in front of you was dressed? Do you nitpick at every little detail and rob yourself and everyone else of the joy of worship? Do you go to church waiting to be spoon fed or do you go to participate in worship?

A woman in a former church calls around to her friends and family every Sunday morning and asks them if they are going "churching" that Sunday. She has it right because she made church a verb. Sunday morning is the worship of our Lord. What we bring to that worship is what we will take away from that worship. We have to make church be a verb. To go "churching" is to actively participate in worship at whatever worship service you can attend. You do not have to jump up and down and shout "amen" but your heart must be open to worship and you must be mentally, emotionally, physically, and soulfully involved in that worship. This is not the time to write a to do list, clean out your purse, text your friends sitting three pews behind you, or worry about what is for dinner. This is not the time to think about what has to be accomplished at work tomorrow or that the lawn needs mowed or the garage needs to be cleaned out.

When we go visit people, we go to their home, sit on their sofa and visit. We focus on them and on our conversation. We actively participate in having a good time and a good visit. When we go to God's house for worship, we need to have the same attitude. In one of my churches we have what we call "Sofa Time." Sofa Time is the opportunity to sit on God's sofa and concentrate on a conversation with God. Some people stay in their pews, some come to the altar, and some come and sit on the first pew. All are concentrating on having a conversation with God.

The other part of "churching" is to be actively involved in ministry. This includes ministry to family and friends and coworkers. This is giving your all at your job as if God were your boss. This is being dedicated to having a good relationship with your spouse and children with God in the midst of it. This is being a good neighbor and a kind coworker. This is being involved in the community and showing God's love and mercy. This is helping at the food pantry, buying the gas for the guy behind you, and offering to babysit for the young couple down the street. Churching is doing for others in such a way that they see that God does love and care for them. Churching is letting people know that they have been noticed, their presence on this earth is acknowledged, and what is happening in their lives matters to someone else.

The verbs that we use to live our lives make us into the people that we become. If we educate ourselves in how to go churching and we practice churching, then it will become obvious to those around us who our Master Instructor is.

Chapter Four Exercises

Exercise One:

A) A great deal of self-defense involves simply being aware of our surroundings. We also need to be aware of ourselves in that environment. For example, knowing where the exits are, where the lights are, or whether or not we are alone can be critical components to being safe. Most of us go about our days without being aware of our surroundings and without being aware or ourselves. We tend to spend little to no time in meditation, soul-checks, and communing with God.

Read slowly and meditate (consider in silence a while before discussing aloud) on the following verses:

Lamentations 3:40

Matthew 7:5

2 Corinthians 13:5

B) Soul-check: After asking each question, sit in silence for about one minute, then discuss aloud.
   1) How is it with your soul?
      a) How is your connection to God, to others, to yourself?

b) What worry or stress is weighing heavily on you?

c) What action, thought, or word performed by you troubles you?

d) What action/thought/word of another troubles you?

e) What emotions have been predominant?

f) What thoughts have been predominant?

g) How does your body feel?

h) Are you able to forgive yourself? Others? Why or why not?

i) Are you able to let go of the troubles? Why or why not?

j) Are you able to trust God? Why or why not?

k) What promises to yourself did you break today? What promises made to others did you break today?

Exercise Two:

A) What are the spiritual disciplines? If you are not familiar with them, a list has been written out by John Wesley. That list can be found in the United Methodist *Book of Discipline* (This is a book written and used by the United Methodist Church.) In the 2008 edition, it is on page 74, ¶103. (See also Ahlberg, *Spiritual Disciplines Handbook* in Resources for Continuing Study.)

B) What of these disciplines are you able to do well?

C) Which disciplines do you struggle with?

D) Why is the practice of the spiritual disciplines important to a healthy spiritual life?

Exercise Three:

A) What is currently happening in your household ? In your neighborhood? In your city? In your state? In your country? In the world?

B) Why is it important for us to be aware of what is happening around us?

C) Which social justice issues do you feel strongly about? If you need a launching point for discussion, the United Methodist *Book of Resolutions* includes a wide range of social justice topics.

D) What are you willing to do to promote a positive change in the issues that you have listed?

E) What have you done recently? What do you plan to do? What do you dream of doing?

SPARRING

EVEN IF IT WAS A BAD FIGHT....

KEY CONCEPT: If you learn something, a bad fight is a good fight.

In karate we will often free fight. In my dojo we use very little padding and just go at it. When fighting a black belt, pretty much anything goes. Certain types of hits and kicks are banned if they lead to death or serious injury. If a black belt is smacked across the nose and has light bursting behind the eyeballs and blood gushing from the nose, the answer is, "Tough, you should have blocked!" There is no whining, no crying, and definitely no finger pointing. Hands are shaken before a fight and after a fight. It is not uncommon to see two blackbelts come off the floor with their arms around each other's necks helping each other stagger to the locker rooms. While they are staggering along, they are mopping up each other's blood and saying things like, "Wow, where did you learn that move?! That was awesome! Will you teach me that one?!" They tape each other up, look after each other's students, and constantly respect each other as human beings.

Someone who is not capable of exhibiting good sportsmanship in these situations is quickly schooled in it. Doing push-ups, running laps, and wall-sitting usually has the desired effect! It goes back to that perfecting bit ....

This translates into everyday life a little too well. We spend a great deal of time neglecting to block and then being unsportsmanlike about it! We have simply lost the ability to accept responsibility for our actions. Along with that ability goes the ability to apologize. We live our lives totally about *us* until it comes to blame time then the focus goes off us as quickly as we can possibly get it off. Instead we focus on our gripes and how we were wronged and "oh, woe are we!!"

We have also lost the fine art of being kind enough to overlook the faults of others. We all make mistakes. Being brutal about the mistakes of others may result in someone being brutal about our mistakes. In order to receive mercy, we must show mercy. We need to teach others how to block. We need to teach others how to live with a blow when they didn't block as well as they should have. It is difficult to be merciful and kind in the face of adversity. There is a big difference in holding someone accountable and being cruel about it. A little kindness goes a long way. We need to help those who find themselves in messy situations for which they are accountable. Burdens are easier to bear when there are more shoulders for the bearing.

Maybe it is time we take a step back and say, "Oops, my bad, I should have blocked." Then we shake hands, shake it off and get to work cleaning it up. The blame game just keeps going around and around. Blame is like a hot potato that no one wants to hold. We want restitution, we want justice, and we want things to go our way. What about mercy, forgiveness, and helping others out?

Each of us lives life as if our life is the only life that is important. We rudely interrupt others, push people out of our way, ignore those who do not meet our lofty expectations (are like us), and in general we have become completely clueless to others unless they are interfering with us getting what we want. We live in a world in which human life simply has no value unless it is our own. This may sound harsh. Remember the whole attitude, humility, respect idea?

For some, this idea may be overstated in regard to the manner in which humanity can behave and for others, it is understated. We are capable of so much more than what we do. I know that forgiveness is exceedingly difficult when someone has hit you below the belt. We get hurt and we get angry and we want the person who made us feel that way feel the same way we do.

I have come to the realization in life that when we are angry what we really are is afraid. We are going to lose something, so we become afraid and we express that fear with anger. We lash out and try to hurt them before they hurt us. The ex-spouse or significant other, the incredibly small-minded, mean-spirited coworkers that must be endured, the boss that won't let up, a family member ..., all of these people affect us and can cause us a great deal of hurt, fear, stress, and anger.

How sportsmanlike are you? Do you block and move on? Do you beat someone into submission literally or figuratively? Do you hatch elaborate plots that will insure their demise, ruin, or just a really bad day? Or, do you take responsibility for the relationship, admit you should have blocked, take the blow, and move on? There is a time and a place for everything. Our lives are less complicated, our souls more at peace if we let the small-minded, mean-spirited, unsportsmanlike people in our lives roll off our backs. When we allow them to constantly anger us and hurt us, we allow them to have control over us. The best revenge in the world, if that is what we are after, is to no longer allow them to have control over us. Riding that emotional roller coaster is a waste of time and energy.

Instead of being tired and discouraged, take some time to discern what can be learned from the situation. What could be done differently? What is the other person afraid of that they treat people (you) the way they do? What in their lives has contributed to their unhappiness and lack of good behavior? What can be done better? How invested in this person are you? What has this incident taught you about that person and about yourself? What can be done? What should be done? What does the Bible say should be done?

Even if we do not win the battle, even if it was an unfair fight, even we are feeling totally miserable, if something was learned then it was not a bad fight. If we gained insight into ourselves and into human nature in general, we have come out ahead. If we have gained insight into the personality of God, we have come out ahead.

Remember that mercy, forgiveness, and grace apply to us as well. Too often, we forgive others more easily than we forgive ourselves. If God does not hold our sins against us, why should we? One of my favorite verses in the Bible is found in Psalms. In Psalm 103:12 we are told that "as far as the east is from the west, God has removed our sins from us." This may not seem all that significant until a little thought is applied. This verse shows the miracle of the Scriptures in our lives today. God knew that in today's technological world, we would have a definitive number for the distance from the North to the South. We have established two distinct poles and know the end points; however, when it comes to east and west, we just keep going around and around and around the planet. The love that is shown to us that God would want us to really understand is that our sins are erased. They have disappeared; they are no more. God has erased them, obliterated them, and forgotten them. Why then, should we, and do we, hang on to them? Dear children of God, let them go; they are gone. Allow yourself to be forgiven. If the Creator of the universe, the Master of the Sea, the Redeemer, the Sustainer of all life lets your sin go, why do you hang on? Let it go.

One of the greatest promises in the Christian life is that every second of every minute of every hour of every day of every week of every month of every year can be a new beginning. With God, there can be a clean slate, a fresh start, new life, new identity, a new leaf, a new creation (2 Corinthians 5:17). We are the only ones who can put on the brakes, not try, wallow in the pits of despair, and never let go. We are the only ones who seem to think that God will do it for others, God is capable of it, but God won't do it for us. God can and God will. There is nothing about you that is so terrible that God will not provide you with the same forgiveness and redemption that is provided to everyone else. There is nothing about you that makes you any more unworthy than anyone else on this planet. John 3:16 is the classic verse to explain this. "For God

so loved the world (that includes you), that He gave His only be-
gotten Son that whoever (that includes you) believes in Him should
not perish but have everlasting life." That life not only is the life
after death that we call Heaven; it is also the life we live now. Life
is a precious gift from God. God wants us to have the best life we
can have, be the best we can be, and have peace and fulfillment
now. We are not to perish spiritually. We are to live. Folks, I encourage you today to choose life. No longer allow your sins and past
failures, your past, your doubts, your shortcomings to hold you
back from life. God created us to live. God alone can and will give
us peace, love, power, mercy, forgiveness, and the best life we can
live right now. All we have to do is choose life.

Let the past go. Remember, we all have bad fights in which we
didn't block. We all have the bruises and scars to show for it. If
there is one thing that all humanity understands it is pain. Jesus
chose the ultimate pain for us so that we could be healed. Jesus
chose to be completely broken so that God's love could flow freely
and fully into a world that was broken. In that brokenness, a miracle took root and the cross became a symbol of hope and love.

Your brokenness today is not in vain. God's love, mercy, forgiveness, and healing can flow unchecked and unhindered when
we are broken just like water can flow unchecked through a broken
pot. The only difference is that while the water eventually runs out,
God's love, mercy, forgiveness, and healing never runs out. Allow
the miracle to take root in the cross that you bear. Allow God to
flow through you and to shine through the brokenness of your
life. Your scars can become symbols of God's love and healing in
your life instead of symbols that justify bitterness and cynicism.
Those scars then become the way in which others can be reached.
Those around us who are hurting and need to know that someone
notices and cares, that God notices and cares, and that they can be
healed. Stop hiding your brokenness. Stop pretending that
everything is under control and you are impervious to the blows
that life inflicts upon us. Let people see the evidence that God
heals, protects, and provides by showing your scars and your lib-
eration into life.

Lesson Five Exercises

EXERCISE ONE:

A) Read and discuss the following verses:

Romans 7:13-20

Ephesians 6:12

1 Peter 5:8

1) Who/what are we fighting against?

2) What is your greatest struggle?

3) What impact does the attitude/actions of others have on your struggle?

EXERCISE TWO:

A) Read and discuss the following verses:

2 Corinthians 10:4

Ephesians 6:10-20

Hebrews 4:12

2 Corinthians 6:7

1 Thessalonians 5:8

1)   What does God equip us with for our fight?

2)   How are each of these used?

3) Which do you use well? Why?

4) Which do you struggle with? Why?

EXERCISE THREE:

A) Read and discuss the following:

Psalm 34:7

Psalm 91:4

Luke 21:18

Psalm 5:11

Psalm 18:2

Psalm 17:8

Proverbs 14:26

Proverbs 30:5

1 John 5:4

Luke 10:19

Romans 8:35-37

Philippians 4:13

2 Corinthians 12:9

1) What are we promised in these verses?

2) Do these promises change how you look at a certain problem/struggle/trial/temptation?

SEEING BEYOND THE PROBLEM

SEE PAST THE TARGET ...

Key Concept: Don't let what you perceive make you stop.

One of the hardest concepts in karate to understand and succeed at is seeing past the target. When we are taught to hit we are taught to visualize our fist or foot coming out the other end of the target. This is the key to breaking boards. It is the natural human way to see the face of the target and view that as the ultimate target. We see the target and we see the hard surface and we stop at that surface. If we stop at the surface of a board, it hurts and the board does not break (which is usually quite embarrassing). If we stop at the surface of a person we do not hit them hard enough to be effective at defending ourselves. The only way to make our hands and feet go through a hard surface is to see past the surface and knowing that it will not stop us.

Too often in life, our problems appear to be so big that we become fairly certain we cannot overcome them. We let our fear and frustration define the problem until we convince ourselves we are unable to win. We quit trying and we fall into the trap of believing we are a helpless victim who is incapable of any kind of victory in this life. Nothing on earth is really that big. Learn to see past the problem. Start looking at the problem, knowing that you will come out the other side. Nothing is completely impenetrable when we have God on our side. Again, quit thinking small when we have a God who is so big. We need to stop thinking that *all we can do is pray* and start realizing that *the best course of action we have is to pray.* God can and will bring us through the problem. Stand on the promises and the power of God. Call down the presence and the power of God and let God take care of the problem.

If it is the kind of problem you cannot go through, ask God to show you the way around it. Sometimes, fighting the problem is not the answer. Sometimes, the answer is going around or over the problem. Sometimes, the answer is to wait. Sometimes, the answer is to do nothing. Sometimes, we cannot fix it and we have to walk away. Sometimes, we have to trust someone else to take care of it and we have to relinquish control.

Stop wasting your energy beating the surface of the problem. Stop bruising your knuckles and bloodying your fingers trying to beat something into the form you want it to be. Start seeing past the problem. Start seeing other alternatives, other avenues. Most of all, start seeing yourself as the victor. Take on the winner mentality and visualize yourself overcoming the problem. Visualize yourself accomplishing the goal. Most of all, know that with God in your corner you are "more than a conqueror" (Romans 8:37).

In Romans 8:31 we are asked a question that we need to learn the answer to: "If God is for us, who can be against us?" Nothing can separate us from God's love, nothing can defeat us, and nothing can destroy us past the point of no return because God can always and will always restore us.

Lesson Six Exercises

EXERCISE ONE:

A) Read and discuss the following:
Isaiah 11:3

2 Corinthians 2:14

1) What is spiritual discernment?

2) How does it play a role in our lives and problems (targets)?

3) In what ways does God provide discernment?

EXERCISE TWO:

A) Read and discuss the following:
2 Thessalonians 1:3

1 Corinthians 13:11

Ephesians 4:13

Hebrews 5:14

1 John 2:14

1) What do these verses tell us about spiritual maturity?

2) Why is spiritual maturity a key part of the discernment process?

3) How do we become more spiritually mature?

4) At what level are you in your spiritual maturity (infant, toddler, tween, teen, etc.)

5) In what ways do you strive to become more spiritually mature?

6) What is your discernment process? How well does it work?

7) What do you need to change about your process? How will you make this change?

EXERCISE THREE:

A) Read and discuss the following verses:
   Matthew 7:24-27

   Matthew 6:19-24

   Matthew 6:25-34

   Isaiah 45:2

   Matthew 21:21

1) In what way does having a solid foundation affect our problem/targets and the way we view them?

2) When reading Matthew 6:25-34, we are reminded that everything in this life is temporary. How do you feel when reminded of this? Does this help you see your problems/targets through a different lens?

3) Matthew 6:25-34 reminds us that God loves us and provides for us. Does this help you not to worry?

4) What sort of problems/targets can you see only the surface of (that you cannot seem to see around)?

5) How do you deal with your worry?

6) How is your ability to deal with worry increased when you read in the scriptures that a way will be provided and that with faith the obstacle (target) can be removed?

KEEPING YOUR KNEES BENT

FALLING OVER? BEND YOUR KNEE ...

Key Concept: Keep your balance.

In karate, balance is everything. Without balance, there is far too much falling and wobbling and general sloppiness. The first concept to having good balance is to have a strong stance. In my art form, we teach three basic stances, all of which have a specific purpose. The one I want to concentrate on now is the one we call the fighting stance. In this stance, our knees are bent, our backs are straight, and our feet are about shoulder-width apart with our toes at specific angles. If this stance is done properly, being knocked over, tripped up, or falling is not going to happen.

From this stance, we gain strength and speed. From this stance, we can fight and defend ourselves. From this stance, we can pop off any technique we need to in order to accomplish whatever our goal is. This stance is important for fighting, for kata, and for feeling our center of balance.

To properly use the stance when fighting we do what we call the "boxer's shuffle." This is bouncing back and forth from one foot to the other while keeping our weight on the balls of our feet. As we bounce our weight back and forth, we are constantly circling our opponent. Movement is the key. Keeping the movement light and quick can mean the difference between winning and losing. The minute the movement becomes heavy and ponderous is the minute the opponent starts to have the upper hand. Stop moving and the fight is lost. Keep the movement light and quick and always move in a circular pattern around the opponent.

To add to the confusion for those of us who are challenged in the coordination department, we have to keep our chins up. We have to keep our backs straight. We have to keep our hands up and our elbows in.

We keep our chins up because we need to see what is coming. This also helps with breathing because as we let our chins fall to our chests we lose the ability to get all the air we can. We keep our hands up so that we protect our face and chest. One hand is for the face and one hand is for the chest. It does no good to have a fabulous stance if we leave our bodies unprotected. We keep our elbows in so that cheap shots to the ribs are not possible.

In Christianity, movement is also a key element in the fight. We have to keep moving by sharing the gospel to the world. We keep moving by standing up to defend our God in a nation of people who want to throw God out. We keep moving by caring for those around us who are oppressed, downtrodden, and beaten by life. We keep moving by staying in touch with God, studying the word of God, and being in a state of constant prayer with God, be it word or action. Remember, this kind of movement is only made possible by the strength of the stance. Power and strength are possible by a powerful and strong stance. We have to decide what our stance will be and stick to it. We have to stand up for what is right, speak out whenever God needs us to, and reach out when someone is falling. Stance is truly crucial to movement. Movement is crucial to the fight. The fight is crucial for lives and souls to be saved. We must choose a stance and stick to it. We must choose a strong stance so we are not knocked over but one that allows us to be flexible enough to do what needs to be done.

In Christianity, we must also keep our chins up. We have to stay current and see what is around us. We cannot afford to live in ignorance and be unaware of what is happening around us. Awareness is crucial to our survival, physically and spiritually. Our hands stay up to protect our bodies. In order to protect ourselves as Christians, we must also keep our hands up. We put up our hands to ask for help whether from another Christian or from our Master. We put up our hands to show praise to God for all that we have and all that we are. We keep up our hands to show our submission to our Master and our willingness to do the work of reaching the world. If our hands are down, not only do we leave ourselves open to unblocked blows, but we are also unable to reach out to anyone or for anyone else.

When we learn to kick, there is a lot of falling. It is hard to learn to trust our bodies to move that way and not end up with our faces on the floor. We try to overcompensate by flailing our arms and shortchanging our kick. The classic rule of thumb is, if you are losing your balance, bend your knee. The knee of the foot that is still on the floor has to be bent. For some reason, we tend to prefer that it be straight even though it means we are going to fall over or have a truly pathetic kick! Not bending our knee can result in personal injury. Either we sprain the knee on the floor or we twist the wrong way in an attempt to torque our bodies enough to pop off a decent kick. We have to bend our knee.

In our Christian lives, balance is everything. Our stance needs to be strong and our bodies centered. The only thing that provides a good foundation, good balance, and a strong stance is the Gospel. We need to study and spend time knowing our God and knowing what God says.

In order to achieve good balance, we need to set priorities. We eat too much junk food and we get sick. We throw off our bodies and do not feel well. We are hungry again quickly and never feel quite full. The sugar makes us sick and thirsty. The calorie overload makes us tired and grumpy.

The spiritual junk food of this world has the same effect on our souls. Too much of all this world has to offer makes us hungry, thirsty, and tired. TV, games, recreation, and fun are all essential to some extent in life. For most, some sort of outlet is truly needed. Balance has to be achieved. Too much of this world throws off our spiritual balance. Whether it is too much work or too much TV, if we are neglecting our soul food, then we are going to start wobbling and falling. We become tired, grumpy, and unhappy.

The best way to achieve this balance is to bend our knees. The only way not to fall is to bend our knees. We often say, "All we can do is pray." We need to start saying, "The best thing we can do is pray."

What happens to us and what concerns us matters deeply to God. We are told that God knows the number of hair on our heads (Luke 12:7), God will wipe away the tears (Isaiah 25:8) and if we have sown tears we will reap with songs of joy (Psalms 126:5). God cares that we lost our job, our spouse, our best friend. God cares that we are lonely or hurting or confused. It matters to God when we lose our favorite toy, shoes, or our faith.

God already knows how we are feeling, so we may as well go ahead and tell God how we feel! I really hate it when I hear people say that we are not to ask God, "Why?" I say that we cannot get an answer without asking a question. When we ask why, we are not challenging God's wisdom, holiness, or supremacy. We just simply need to understand what we are to do, what we are to learn, and where we are to go from here. Bend your knees. Keep your balance and bend your knees. More importantly, in order to keep your balance, bend your knees.

When learning to kick, one of the secrets that is soon learned is that the knee is pointed at the target regardless of the kind of kick that will be done. Kicks always are performed by knee, foot, knee sequences. The leg that is doing the kicking is pulled up and bent, the knee is pointed at the target, and then the foot comes out to perform the kick. The knee is bent again and the leg comes back to ready position. Pointing the knee at the target ensures that the target will be hit. Praying is the only way to ensure that the target is hit. The target can be a problem or a praise. The target can be a feeling or a failure. The target can be a habit or an emergency. Regardless of what the target may be, remember to bend you knee and point it at the target.

The next time the knee is bent is when returning to ready position. So the knee is bent again after dealing with the target or the problem. After returning to ready position, the knees remain bent.

We must pray before the problem, during the problem, and then after the problem.

Talk to God; then listen for the answer. Be still, be silent and listen for the voice of your Master. Your Master will not let you down. Be patient; the answer comes in the Master's time. Be able to keep your stance and fight; bend your knees.

A) BREATHE IN THROUGH THE NOSE AND OUT THROUGH THE MOUTH.

Key Concept: Breathe …

When we start sparring, we also have to learn to breathe. If you cannot breathe, you cannot fight. It is essential to breathe in through the nose and out through the mouth. It is essential to breathe out whenever taking a hit. It is much easier on the body to breathe out the air than to have it knocked out!

Sucking and gasping for air is truly no fun. That feeling of being hit below the belt and having the wind knocked out of you is not a good feeling. Being fairly certain that your oxygen supply just got limited is pretty scary. Most of the time, in a fight there is no time to stop and catch your breath. So breathe to begin with!

In our Christian discipline, we have this thing called prayer. Prayer can be described as talking to God. Prayer also includes all of our thoughts, actions, and conversations with other Christians.

A discipline that is helpful in prayer is known as "breath prayers." A breath prayer is a private prayer; it is that intimate moment between you and God. There are a variety of breath prayers available. Many denominations have ones that are commonly used throughout the day. Breath prayers are any prayers that are prayed frequently though out the day. A good example is what is known as the "Jesus prayer" or "the prayer of the heart." This prayer merely states, "Lord Jesus Christ, Son of God, have mercy on me a poor lost sinner." This prayer can be repeated throughout the day. Why is it important? It provides focus. There is acknowledgment of who Jesus is, who we are, and that our help comes from Jesus.

It is not uncommon for people to write their own breath prayers. To do this just pick a phrase that is meaningful to you personally. It could be scripture or any phrase that provides focus and a realization of the presence of God. Some of the words are said when breathing in and the rest are said when breathing out. All that is needed are short sentences with the intention of focusing on God and God's presence in our lives. An acknowledgment of where our help and hope come from.

What are your favorite names for God? Creator, Redeemer, Sustainer, Emmanuel, The Great Physician, Jehovah, Lord, and Savior are a few examples to help you get started.

What is the way you acknowledge God's presence in your life? The Bible, nature, the face of a loved one, children playing, music are all ways to help you focus.

How do you ask for guidance and help? The Psalms are an excellent resource for providing ways not only to ask for help but to praise God and what God has done for you.

By breathing on a regular basis, we don't have as much air knocked out of us when we take a blow. By breathing on a regular basis, we minimize the damage when we take a blow. By praying on a regular basis, we are better able to handle the blows dealt to us on a daily basis. By praying on a regular basis, we have heard the voice of our Master and we know that voice when there is trouble. When we know that voice, we can hear the answer. When we know the Master, we often know what the answer is going to be. We are better able to cope with life, stress, and hard below-the-belt hits. Go ahead: breathe!

Lesson Seven Exercises

EXERCISE ONE:

In the martial arts world, the best fighting stance requires a step out and bent knees. When this stance is assumed, strength and balance are increased. When we are fighting for our balance, it is usually because our knees are either not bent at all or not bent far enough. Breathing is also crucial to fighting. If we have no breath we cannot fight. In our spiritual fights, we must take a step out. We simply cannot be non-active participants in the Christian faith and be effective. We must also keep our knees bent. Prayer is the cornerstone for the Christian faith. Without prayer and constant communion with God (not just the laundry list of the problems, sick, troubles, etc.) we quickly flounder and fall over. Prayer should be on every breath in our lives. We should literally be in such a close relationship with God that even as we go about the tasks that are necessary in this world, we are in prayer.

A) Read and discuss the following:

Luke 11:9

John 15:7

Psalm 91:15

2 Chronicles 7:14

James 5:16

1) Are there conditions to prayer? If so, what are they?

2) God promises to always answer our prayers. What prayers have you had answered?

3) Are there any prayers that you think were not answered? Why or why not?

4) Does prayer play a vital role in your life? How?

EXERCISE TWO:

A) Read and discuss the following:
Mark 1:35

Mark 6:46, 47

Luke 5:15, 16

Luke 6:12

Numbers 20:6

1 Kings 8:54

Exodus 4:31

1 Kings 8:22

Matthew 6:5-8, 14, 15

1) What do these scriptures teach us about prayer?

2) What is prayer?

3) Are you comfortable with prayer? Why or why not?

4) If you are not, what do you need to do to become comfortable with prayer (this does not refer only to public prayer)?

EXERCISE THREE:

A) Many folks today hire a life coach to help them with decisions and to teach them how to live the best life possible. A life coach can act as moral guide, schedule keeper, cheerleader, parent, etc. Whatever a person needs to live life well, a life coach will help them to write out a life plan and to carry it out. Read Matthew 6:9-13.

1) Using the Lord's Prayer as a guide, write out a life plan for yourself.

2) What help do you need to live out this life plan?

EXERCISE FOUR:

A) In several classes in seminary when working on prayer, we were taught about breath prayers. A breath prayer says all you need to say to God in any one given second repeatedly throughout the day. One phrase of the prayer is said when breathing in and the second phrase is said when breathing out. An example might be, "Lord, you are my all in all (while breathing in), guide me, lead me, I am yours (while breathing out)." The phrases should not be too long; they only need to be a few syllables.

Write a breath prayer for yourself. Begin to practice saying that breath prayer several times a day.

GOD HAS OUR BACK

YOU HAVE TWO HANDS...

Key Concept: We are not alone.

So, we know who we are, we are balanced, breathing and ready to go. How else do we win our battles? Well, God gave us a gift to provide us with guidance and answers. We have at our disposal the Holy Spirit. We have a coach, if you will, that is constantly at our side encouraging us and guiding us.

There is a defense move that is one of my favorites. I will try to describe it to you to show you how when the power and the presence of the Holy Spirit enters into a situation, everything changes. When someone grabs your wrist, it is really fairly simple to get away. All you do is twist your arm toward their thumb while you pull away. If you break the thumb from the hold, they cannot keep hold of you. We, as humans, need our thumbs to keep a grip on anything.

If they grab onto your wrist with both hands, it can be anywhere from difficult to impossible to just twist away from the hold. However, if you bring your other arm up to grab the hand of the other arm and pull up, you can break the hold. While the hand on the bottom pushes up, the hand on top pulls. With both hands working together the hold of the thumbs of the opponent can be broken. You see, one handed you cannot do it.

Using both hands is a constant in karate. All of our blocks require both hands. We use both hands to cross the body. Then while one hand finishes the block, the other hand comes to ready position at the waist in order to punch. We always follow a block with a punch. We need to gain this mindset as Christians. We tend to just dodge our problems, avoid them, and hope they will go away. We are seldom actively fighting those problems.

By ourselves, any problem that presents itself can be difficult to deal with. We succeed sometimes and sometimes we fail. Most problems will rear their ugly heads repeatedly until we call in rein- forcements. For us, that is the Holy Spirit. We tap into the power of God by calling the Holy Spirit into our lives, our problems, and our churches. Everything changes when we are not doing it alone. The Holy Spirit is the other arm. We no longer have to twist and struggle on our own with every problem that comes our way. We are no longer alone. You are no longer alone. You have the power of God at your disposal; you have the promise of the constant presence and hope of God. You have the other arm. You are not alone.

I tell students that if you want to come out of the hold with a little attitude, after you have pulled upward and freed yourself, bend your elbow and keep going. That lovely bent elbow leaves quite an impression when placed along the face of your attacker on the way up! Go ahead, have a little attitude about it! You can break free of whatever holds you. With the Holy Spirit in your life, you are no longer a prisoner to your past, your sins, your habits, or your ad- dictions. It may not be an easy journey. It may not be a quick fight. But the fight can be won when we do not fight alone.

Lesson Eight Exercises

EXERCISE ONE:

A) Review the promises of God in Lesson Three. List the promises that include God being with us.

B) Review the promises of God in Lesson Five. List the promises that include God's protection.

C) Review the promises of God in Lesson Six. List the promises of God that show God's immediate involvement in our lives and circumstances.

    1)   List times/places in your life when you have felt alone.

    2)   Does this list change when you review all of God's promises of protection and presence?

    3)   What are you afraid of?

    4)   Is it at times of fear that you feel most alone? Why or why not?

EXERCISE TWO:

A) Read and discuss the following:
Ephesians 2:11-22

Ephesians 4:2-6

Galatians 6:1-10

1) What do these passages of scripture tell us about being a member of the Body of Christ?

2) How should we be treating each other?

3) In what ways do you contribute to the Body of Christ?

4) In what ways could you contribute more to the Body of Christ?

5) In what ways could you improve your involvement in the Body of Christ?

6) In what ways are you actively involved in bearing another's burdens or being a presence in someone's life so that they know they are not alone?

EXERCISE THREE:

A) Read and discuss Luke 15:1-10

1) What does the Parable of the Lost Sheep show us about how God is with us and cares for us?

2) In what ways have you turned your back and left the fold of God?

3) In what ways have you felt God's presence even with your back turned?

4) In what ways have you felt and experienced restoration with God and the Body of Christ?

5) In what ways do you need to be restored?

6) What does the Parable of the Lost Coin show us about restoration with God?

7) The woman in the parable cleaned house in search of what she had lost. Restoration occurred after she actively participated in the work of restoration. What do you need to clean out or do to actively participate in the restoration that God has promised? What do you need to remove? Is there bitterness, anger, unforgiveness, hatred, etc., that needs to be dealt with on your part before you can experience full restoration?

8) What help do you need from God for that restoration to take place?

9) What help do you need from the Body of Christ for that restoration to take place?

10) Find scripture that promises us the hope of eternal life, of a future hope, and of being part of more than what the world offers.

EXERCISE FOUR:

IN CONCLUSION......

Just as in karate we must do the same motions over and over again to make them become a habit, so too must you constantly repeat the motions provided for you in this study. Becoming a strong and active participant in the Body of Christ takes dedicated practice and endurance. Being a disciple of Christ requires a life of routine motions that will become habits and life skills.

The hope I have when teaching students what they need to know is that those motions, thoughts, and abilities will become such an ingrained habit that when needed, they act before they panic and save their lives and the lives of others. The hope I have in this study is that you will have these motions, thoughts, and abilities become such ingrained habits that when life gets hard and messy you do not panic, but you do what is needed to get through it in the manner that God hopes and provides for us.

The biggest lesson to learn is that we have to take part in what God does for us. God grants a lot of unexpected, miraculous moments and miracles in life; however, much of the Christian life requires our active participation in order for what has been provided to be effective for us. I can teach all the fancy moves I want to students but unless they are committed to it, practice it, and then give it all they have when they need to, it does them no good.

In order to get the most out of what God has promised and provided for us, we must practice it, be committed to it, and give it our all.

Blessings to you in your journey and practice. Getting discouraged and tired is a normal human reaction, so I encourage you to find Sabbath time to rest, renew, and enjoy God. Sabbath in today's world is hard to do but again, it requires dedication, practice, and participation on our parts to make finding time work.

Remember, we are not victims, we are not survivors, we are not even conquerors, because with God we are MORE than conquerors through Christ who loves us. Amen.

AFTERWORD

Shauna Hyde is a living example that we control our response to circumstances rather than allowing our circumstances to control us. As a woman of faith and strength, Shauna has used her experiences to deepen her faith in Christ and to empower other persons to tap into the deep resources of faith and strength that is available for us.

She continues her ministry of empowerment here as one of the pastors of the Christ Church community. Women and men alike have been empowered to draw upon the deep resources available within and to live out their lives as strong people of faith.

Through her presence, her leadership and her joy, she is an example of the life she encourages others to live. It is my joy to call her my colleague and friend.

Dr. Randall F. Flanagan
Lead Pastor
Christ Church United Methodist

RESOURCES FOR CONTINUING STUDY

Below is a list of books that I hope will help you continue to study and grow. This list is varied in topics, authors, and work levels. My prayer is that each of you will continue to understand what God has empowered us to do and to become. Education and practice are tools to that understanding. This is by no means a comprehensive list. I had to set a limit for myself so as not to overwhelm you with resources! Once you begin the journey, you will find more resources and I ask you to share them with others and with me.

Ahlberg, Adele. *Spiritual Disciplines Handbook: Practices That Transform Us.* Downer's Grove, IL: IVP Books, 2005 (ISBN 9780830833306).

Beattie, Melody. *Codependent No More.* Center City, MN: Hazelden Foundation, 1992 (ISBN 0894864025).

Clairmont, Patsy. *Sportin' a 'Tude.* Carol Stream, IL: Tyndale House Publishers, 1996 (ISBN 1561796468).

Clinebell, Howard. *Anchoring Your Well Being.* Claremont, CA: Howard Clinebell, 1997 (ISBN 0835808211).

Cloud, Dr Henry and Dr John Townsend. *Boundaries: When to Say YES, When to Say NO, To Take Control of Your Life.* Grand Rapids, MI: Zondervan, 1992 (ISBN 0310585902).

Copeland, Deb. *Attitude Therapy.* Bloomington, IN: AuthorHouse Publishers, 2006 (ISBN 9781425957902).

Crabb, Dr. Larry. *Inside Out.* Colorado Springs, CO: Navpress, 1988 (ISBN 1576830829).

Howe, Leroy T. *Guilt: Helping God's People Find Healing and Forgiveness.* Nashville: Abingdon Press, 2003 (ISBN 068702594X).

Lyght, Ernest, Glory E. Dharmaraj, and Jacob S. Dharmaraj. *Many Faces One Church.* Nashville: Abingdon Press, 2006 (ISBN 0687494451).

Miles, Reverend Al. *Domestic Violence: What Every Pastor Needs to Know.* Minneapolis, MN: Augsburg Fortress, 2000 (ISBN 0800631757).

Mittelberg, Mark. *The Questions Christians Hope No One Will Ask.* Carol Stream, IL: Tyndale House Publishers, 2010 (ISBN 9781414315911).

Nelson, Rev. Gary E. *A Relentless Hope: Surviving the Storm of Teen Depression.* Eugene, OR: Wipf and Stock Publishers, 2007 (ISBN 9781556353093). http://www.survivingteendepression.com.

Nouwen, Henri J.M. *The Return of the Prodigal Son: A Story of Homecoming.* Garden City, NY: Image Books, 1992 (ISBN 0385473079).

Park, Andrew Sung. *From Hurt to Healing: A Theology of the Wounded.* Nahsville: Abingdon Press, 2004 (ISBN 0687038812).

Sande, Ken. *The Peace Maker: A Biblical Guide to Resolving Conflict.* Grand Rapids, MI: BakerBooks, 2004 (ISBN 9780801064852).

Smith, Edward M. *Healing Life's Deepest Hurts.* Ann Arbor, MI: New Creation Publishing and Vine Books/Servant Publications, 2002 (ISBN 156955346).

Smith, Harold Ivan. *A Long-Shadowed Grief: Suicide and its Aftermath.* Lanham, MI: Cowley Publications, 2006 (ISBN 9781561012817).

Stone, Howard W. *Defeating Depression.* Minneapolis, MN: Augsburg Books, 2007 (ISBN 9780806690315).

You might also like ...

Most of doing church happens outside the building
— or it should!

Join the story! Learn practical lessons from
Old Testament passages.

More from Energion Publications

Personal Study

The Jesus Paradigm	$17.99
Finding My Way in Christianity	$16.99
When People Speak for God	$17.99
Holy Smoke, Unholy Fire	$14.99
Not Ashamed of the Gospel	$12.99
Evidence for the Bible	$16.99
Christianity and Secularism	$16.99
What's In A Version?	$12.99
The Messiah and His Kingdom to Come	$19.99 (B&W)

Christian Living

52 Weeks of Ordinary People – Extraordinary God	$7.99
Daily Devotions of Ordinary People – Extraordinary God	$19.99
Directed Paths	$7.99
Grief: Finding the Candle of Light	$8.99
I Want to Pray	$7.99
Rite of Passage for the Home and Church	$13.99
Soup Kitchen for the Soul	$12.99

Bible Study

Learning and Living Scripture	$12.99
To the Hebrews: A Participatory Study Guide	$9.99
Revelation: A Participatory Study Guide	$9.99
The Gospel According to St. Luke: A Participatory Study Guide	$8.99
Identifying Your Gifts and Service: Small Group Edition	$12.99
Why Four Gospels?	$11.99

Theology

God's Desire for the Nations	$18.99
Operation Olive Branch	$16.99
Christian Archy	$9.99
Ultimate Allegiance	$9.99
The Politics of Witness	$9.99

Generous Quantity Discounts Available

Dealer Inquiries Welcome

Energion Publications

P.O. Box 841

Gonzalez, FL 32560

Website: http://energionpubs.com

Phone: (850) 525-3916

CPSIA information can be obtained at www.ICGtesting.com
Printed in the USA
LVOW040338021111

253135LV00002B/23/P